BILL
DANCE'S

FISHING TIPS

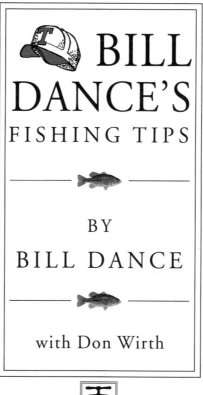

BILL DANCE'S
FISHING TIPS

BY

BILL DANCE

with Don Wirth

PREMIUM PRESS AMERICA
NASHVILLE, TN

BILL DANCE'S FISHING TIPS by Bill Dance and Don Wirth
Published 1998 by PREMIUM PRESS AMERICA.
Copyright © 1998 by Don Wirth

ISBN 1-887654-46-1

Library of Congress Catalog Card Number applied for

PREMIUM PRESS AMERICA books are available at special discounts
for premiums, sales promotions, fund-raising, or educational use. For
details contact the Publisher at P.O. Box 159015, Nashville, TN
37215, or phone toll free (800) 891-7323 or (615) 256-8484.

Cover design by Jeremy Wirth
Interior design and original artwork by Bob Bubnis/BookSetters
Printed by Vaughan Printing
Cover photo by Pete McClure

First Edition 1998
1 2 3 4 5 6 7 8 9 10

About The Authors

BILL DANCE is truly "America's Favorite Fisherman." His TNN television show, "Bill Dance Outdoors," is America's most popular fishing program. This Memphis, Tenn. native became a nationally-prominent bass angler during organized tournament fishing's formative period in the late Sixties-early Seventies. A naturally-gifted bass angler, he quickly made his mark as one of the sport's pioneer structure fishermen, and was among the first to popularize structure-fishing concepts and methods among the angling public. During his illustrious tournament-fishing career, Dance won 13 national bass titles and was named the Bass Anglers Sportsman Society's Angler of the year twice. His prowess with the plastic worm is legendary; Dance won many important tournaments on this lure and helped introduce it to anglers across America. Dance has devoted the years following his retirement from the cast-for-cash circuit to educating fishermen, and has taught his proven angling techniques to millions through his television and radio broadcasts, books, videos, magazine articles and seminars at leading universities. Dance has traveled across North America in pursuit of virtually every species of freshwater gamefish and is adept at catching everything from pond bluegills to giant stripers. His patented recipe of useful information presented in a down-to-earth, entertaining manner is evident in the tips he's personally selected for this book.

DON WIRTH of Nashville, Tenn. is one of America's most prolific freelance outdoor journalists. His award-winning fishing features and colorful photography appear regularly in such popular publications as *BASSMASTER, BASSIN', NORTH AMERICAN FISHERMAN* and *FISHING FACTS.* Wirth is also an accomplished video and music producer and a consultant to the fishing and boating industries. A veteran multispecies angler and keen observer of the fishing scene, his no-nonsense writing style is a perfect compliment to Bill Dance's vast storehouse of fishing information.

BASS BACKGROUND
Fascinating Facts About America's Favorite Gamefish

Largemouth Bass

The largemouth bass lives in every state except Alaska, and in many foreign countries. It prefers shallow lakes and ponds, timber-filled reservoirs and slow-moving rivers, where it can often be found near submerged logs, brush and vegetation. Largemouth bass eat a menu of prey which include minnows, small bluegills and crayfish, and will aggressively attack a broad array of artificial lures. The world record largemouth bass was caught in Montgomery Lake, Ga. and weighed 22 lb. 4 oz.

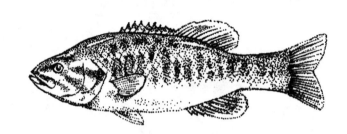

Smallmouth Bass

The smallmouth bass has a preference for cool water, which helps account for its more limited range. It favors deep, clear lakes and reservoirs and fast-flowing rivers and streams, where it prowls rocky banks and gravel bars for crayfish and minnows. Pound for pound, the smallmouth is arguably the hardest-fighting member of the bass clan. The world record smallmouth bass came from Dale Hollow Lake, Tenn. and weighed 10 lb. 14 oz.

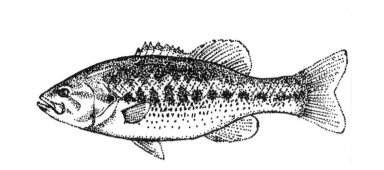

Spotted Bass

The spotted or Kentucky bass looks like a brightly-colored largemouth, but, like the smallmouth, prefers clear, rocky reservoirs and rivers. It often suspends in open water and has been reported to live as deep as 100 feet. This hard-hitting bass is most easily caught on small lures that mimic minnows and crayfish. The world record spotted bass was taken from Pine Flat Lake, Cal. and weighed 9 lb. 7 oz.

BASS FISHING TIPS

A Few Good Lures

There are thousands of different bass lures on the market, but
you only need a few to consistently catch bass. Jigs, spinnerbaits, crankbaits, plastic worms and topwater lures will catch
bass wherever these great gamefish swim. Other lures will work,
too, but always keep these basic baits in the top drawer of your
tacklebox.

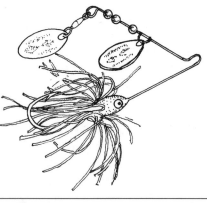

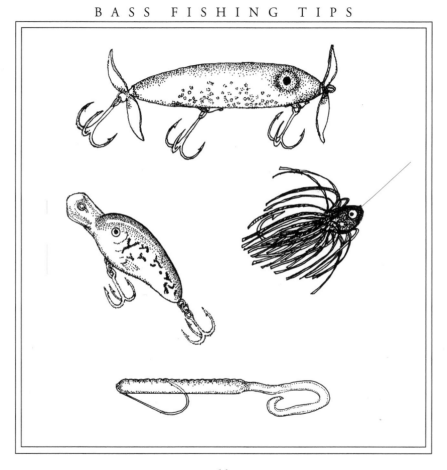

Water Temperature And Bass Activity

Bass are cold-blooded creatures, so their activity level is directly related to the temperature of their surroundings. If the water is below 60 degrees, fish slow-moving lures like jigs and plastic worms close to the bottom. In warmer water, faster-moving lures like crankbaits and spinnerbaits fished off the bottom will usually work better.

How Clear Is The Water?

Water clarity will also help determine which lure to use. In clear water, bass can see your lure easily, so use realistic offerings like minnow imitators or plastic worms. In murky water, bass rely less on their eyes and more on their lateral line, which senses vibrations made by prey moving through the water. If the water appears stained or muddy, use lures like spinnerbaits, crankbaits and jigs that vibrate, click or rattle when retrieved.

Which Lure Color Is Best?

Bass can see colors about as well as humans can. In clear water, use realistic lure colors that mimic living prey—silver or gold crankbaits and topwater plugs, black or brown jigs. In murky water, use bright colors that can be easily seen, such as chartreuse crankbaits or white spinnerbaits.

Jig 'N' Pig For Big Bass

A jig 'n' pig (jig with pork or soft plastic trailer) is arguably the best of all big-bass lures. When bumped across the bottom, it looks and moves much like a live crayfish. For largemouths, fish a rubber-legged jig with a large pork or soft plastic trailer around shallow logs, stumps and weedbeds. For smallmouths and spotted bass, move out deeper and try a jig with a small frog chunk in rocky areas.

Lures That Rattle

When crayfish crawl across the bottom, they make a clicking sound which bass recognize as a feeding cue. A jig or crankbait with built-in rattles will simulate this sound.

Four Seasons Of Bassin'

Bass often display strong seasonal habitat preferences. In spring, they prefer shallow bays and tributaries protected from cold north winds. In summer, they gravitate to dropoffs, ledges and submerged vegetation. In fall, they prowl coves, main-lake points, submerged islands and other offshore structures. In winter, look for them on deep points, sloping banks and channel ledges.

Where To Find The Warmest Water

In early spring, look for the warmest water if you're serious about latching into a lunker bass. You'll usually find both in the northwest corner of the lake. Cold northerly winds blow over this area, and it receives more sunlight, making the water here as much as 5 degrees warmer than elsewhere in the lake.

Weeds And Bass

Aquatic vegetation is tremendous habitat for largemouth bass. It filters impurities from the water, produces oxygen, attracts minnows and crayfish and serves as an excellent hiding place. Fish weedless lures around submerged grass, lilypads, hydrilla and other vegetation.

Target The First And Last Weeds

Aquatic vegetation, like other living things in the water, has a life cycle. Try to locate the first weeds to appear in early spring and the last ones to die off in late fall, for bass will often congregate around them in large numbers.

Spring Rains Pull Bass Shallow

Heavy rains may warm the water in a reservoir overnight in early spring. When this happens, bass often move out of deep water and head for shallow mud banks to gorge on crayfish emerging from their winter hibernation. A brown or green crankbait rooted along the bottom will mimic a fleeing crayfish and should draw strikes.

Crank The Mudline

A mudline created by wave action against the shoreline is a great place to catch bass in a clear lake. Bass move into this murky band of water to feed on crayfish uprooted by the churning waves, and will nail a crankbait.

Farm Pond Lunkers

Some of the biggest largemouth bass caught every year come from farm ponds. Pond bass typically receive little fishing pressure and can grow to large size quickly. Try spinnerbaits, plastic worms, jigs and topwater lures around submerged wood cover, weedy shorelines and any depth change, especially one close to the bank.

Sneak Up On Pond Bass

Use a stealthy approach when fishing a clear pond—often the bass can see you before you see them. Avoid brightly-colored shirts and hats; experienced pond anglers often wear camouflaged clothing. Direct your first casts close to the shoreline while you are still a good distance away from the water's edge.

The Eyes Have It

In clear water, the success of artificial lures often declines during the middle of the day. Bass can scrutinize lures more easily during this high-light period, and, since no lure looks 100% real, will often reject them. Live bait fishermen, on the other hand, tend to do better during the middle of the day than lure casters—what could look more real to a bass than living prey?

Minnow Mimic

A minnow being pursued by a bass doesn't swim lazily, it darts this way and that trying to escape. To more effectively mimic a a live minnow when using a crankbait, bump the lure off a rock, stump or the bottom. This alters its speed and direction and makes it look more like a fleeing baitfish to a hungry bass.

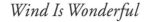

Wind Is Wonderful

Most fishermen try to get out of the wind, but this can be a big mistake. The wind often blows plankton into shallow water. Plankton-eating baitfish such as threadfin shad will move onto windy banks to feed, and bass will be close behind. Try silvery crankbaits, grubs and topwater lures close to shore.

The Versatile Worm

A plastic worm is one of the most versatile lures you can use for bass. In lakes with lots of shallow wood or weeds, rig it Texas-style and fish it tight to cover. In clear reservoirs where most bass live offshore, rig it Carolina-style and fish it on points, submerged humps and dropoffs. In deep, rocky lakes, use a small finesse worm on a splitshot rig or leadhead, leaving the hook point exposed.

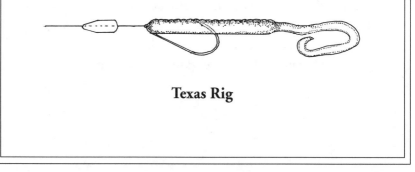

Texas Rig

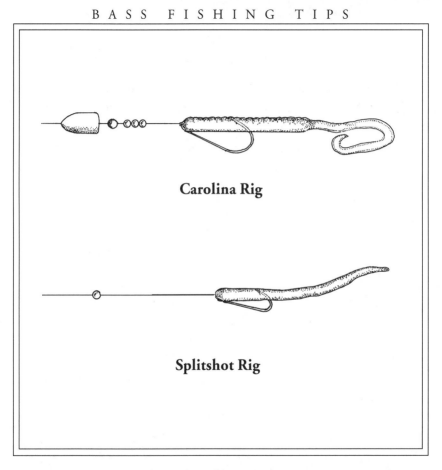

Carolina Rig

Splitshot Rig

Buzz Up A Bass

A buzz bait doesn't look very realistic when you hold it in your hand, but when you retrieve it across the surface, its noisy, sputtering action looks remarkably like a frog skittering frantically across the surface. No wonder pro bassers favor buzzers for big bass!

Spoon Feed Offshore Bass

In deep, clear lakes and reservoirs, the absence of shallow wood or weed cover may cause bass to spend much of the year offshore. Use your depth finder to locate large schools of baitfish off points and dropoffs. Dropping a shiny metal spoon straight down into this baitfish school and jigging it repeatedly will often nail a bass.

Sometimes Smaller Is Better

When the bass bite is slow, try downsizing your lures. A 4-inch plastic worm fished across the bottom on a simple splitshot rig will draw plenty of strikes even when other lures and presentations fail.

Spawning Bass Tips

Largemouth bass spawn in shallow bays and tributaries protected from cold winds and wave action when the water reaches approximately 70 degrees in spring. Their nest appears as a light-colored patch on the bottom. Sight-fishing for spawning bass is exciting—wear Polarized sunglasses and bump a small plastic worm or tube bait through the nest, setting the hook the instant the bass takes the bait. Always release any spawning bass you catch immediately so they can complete their nesting cycle.

Use The Right Spinnerbait

Not all spinnerbaits are created equal. Use a willow-leaf spinnerbait in clear water—its long, slender blades look like live baitfish. Try a spinnerbait with Colorado blades in murky water, or at night. Its rounded, heavily-cupped blades produce heavy vibrations that help bass zero in on the lure with their lateral line in low-visibility conditions.

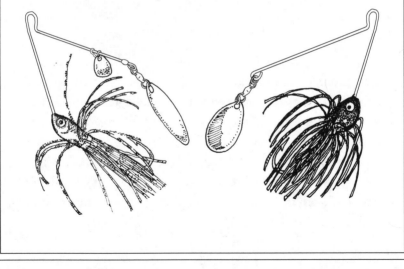

Frogs, Rats & Big Bass

Try weedless plastic frogs or rats skipped erratically across the top of lilypads or matted surface weeds for summer bass. When a bass strikes the frog, immediately drop the rod tip and let the fish pull the line tight before setting the hook hard. Be patient— jerking back immediately will usually pull the frog away from the fish. Wait until you feel the fish before striking.

How To Cast Frogs & Rats Farther

Weedless frogs and rats are lightweight lures that should be fished on heavy tackle. To make them easier to cast on stout baitcasting gear without adversely affecting their floatation, slice an opening in the top of the bait and cram pieces of plastic worm inside. Adding a noisy glass worm rattle or two will help the bass zero in on the lure in heavy cover.

One-Two Punch

When fishing a buzz bait, keep a second rod rigged with a "fall-back lure" on standby. If a bass rolls on the buzzer and misses it, immediately cast a floating plastic worm or soft jerk bait to the spot—the fish will usually strike it.

Jerking Big Bass

In early spring, bass often "stage" or hold on dropoffs close to spawning areas, where they wait until the water warms before moving shallow to spawn. A suspending "jerk bait" (weighted minnow imitator) is a good choice for these staging bass. Cast it well off the bank, let it sink several feet, jerk the rod tip once or twice, then allow the lure to sink again while taking up slack with the reel. Bass usually strike the bait between jerks. If you feel a weight on the line after reeling up slack line, don't set the hook too hard—you may pull the lure's small hooks out of the fish. Instead, turn the reel handle quickly to "tighten down" on the bass. The fish will usually hook itself when it feels resistance and tries to escape.

Stream Savvy

Small streams can hold some surprisingly big bass. Slow-moving streams with murky water are best for largemouths, while small-mouth and spotted bass can abound in clear streams with swift current. Often the best way to fish a stream is to wade it. Wade upstream and retrieve your lures in the direction of the current.

Minnow Mimics

Leadhead grubs and finesse worms are ideal stream lures. They mimic small minnows stream bass feed upon, and they're inexpensive to replace should you break them off in an underwater snag.

Keeping Current

Current can play a major role in determining bass location in a river or stream. Largemouth bass don't care for current and will usually locate in slack water, or very close to current-deflecting objects including sunken logs, rocks or bridge pilings. Smallmouth and spotted bass, on the other hand, are perfectly at home in current and more likely than largemouths to rush out into fast water to chase down a meal.

Determine A Pattern

When fishing a new lake, first concentrate on a small area, such as a bay or tributary, to determine a viable pattern. If you find bass holding on, for example, isolated stumps in 6 feet of water, you can then catch fish elsewhere on the lake by locating these same conditions in other areas.

Bump Cover For Big Bass

One of the easiest ways to increase both the quantity and quality of the bass you catch is to make sure your lure contacts cover when you retrieve it. Bumping the lure off a hard submerged object such as a rock, stump or tree limb will cause the bait to suddenly change speed and direction, just as a live crayfish or baitfish would if pursued by a bass.

Bass Hotspots

An underwater spring can be a hotspot for bass during the winter months. Spring water will be significantly warmer than the surrounding lake water, and will attract large numbers of baitfish and bass. Spring water is often extremely clear, so fish it with your most realistic artificial lures or use live bait.

Fish The Edges

Bass gravitate to edges—places where one type of habitat meets another. The bottom, shoreline and surface are primary edges; baitfish and other forage species often gather in these locations in large quantities, creating excellent feeding opportunities for bass. Other common edges include places where cover such as a stump row or weedline meets open water, dropoffs, areas where ditches or channels intersect flats, and the end of a long point. When in doubt about where to fish, it's always a safe bet to try the lake's edges first.

Stop And Go

When retrieving a crankbait, avoid reeling the bait straight in—this gives it a mechanical, unrealistic look. Instead, vary the retrieve speed and stop the lure occasionally for a more natural presentation.

Float A Worm

In late spring, water in reservoirs often rises to flood shoreline bushes. A floating plastic worm rigged with a weedless hook is a deadly sight-fishing lure around this shallow cover. Use open-face spinning gear to present the worm close to cover, and watch for bass moving out of the bushes to strike. A high-visibility pink, orange or chartreuse floating worm often provokes a reaction strike from bass.

Shock Absorber

When fishing a crankbait, use a long, flexible rod. This allows you to cast the lure a greater distance and also acts as a shock absorber, preventing a lightly-hooked bass from pulling the hooks free.

Keep On Truckin'

If a bass strikes your surface bait and misses, don't freeze—keep working it back to the boat with the same retrieve you were using. The bass may strike at a moving topwater lure several times before finally connecting.

Feeding Frenzy

In summer and fall, large schools of bass often chase baitfish to the top in a feeding frenzy. To locate active bass schools, cruise

the lake and watch for circling and diving birds—they're feeding on the injured baitfish the bass have left behind.

The Deadly Grub

A leadhead grub is an often-overlooked bass lure. It's especially
deadly on smallmouth and spotted bass. Rig the grub with
hook exposed, cast it to points or flats and let it sink to the bottom. Then hold the rod tip at 10 o'clock and reel slowly, stopping every few yards to let it fall, then swimming the grub just
off the bottom. When a bass inhales it, set the hook.

Fine-Tune With Color

Use color to fine-tune your lure presentation. If bass in mod-
erately murky water aren't responding to a black plastic worm,

try a black worm with a hot- colored tail—adding this small amount of bright color will help make your lure more easily-noticed by bass without making it look totally unnatural.

Don't Spook Wary Bass

When fishing shallow areas, set your electric trolling motor on a slow to moderate speed and keep it there. This is less likely to alert wary bass of your presence than if you repeatedly started and stopped the motor.

A Subtle Tip For Clear Water

In clear water, contrasting dark colors can be combined to make your lure more visible without making it appear unnatural—for example, fish a black hair jig with a brown pork trailer.

Nature's Signs

Pay attention to Nature's signs when you're fishing. If you see plenty of active birds or game on the surrounding shores, chances are the bass will be active, too.

Horizontal Vs. Vertical Lures

Begin your search for actively-feeding bass with lures that move horizontally through the water column at a moderate to fast speed, including spinnerbaits, crankbaits, jerk baits and surface lures. If these don't work, slow down and fish lures that drop to the bottom, including jigs, plastic worms and leadhead grubs.

Weed Detector

Use a diving crankbait to detect deep weedbeds on points and submerged islands. Make a long cast and dredge the bait across bottom; if it comes back with weeds, retrieve a Carolina-rigged plastic worm or weedless jig through this spot.

Skim The Surface

Skim the top of weedbeds growing just beneath the surface of the water with a fast-moving lure such as a buzz bait or lipless crankbait. Often this will provoke a reaction strike from bass holed up in the vegetation below.

Do Nothing To Catch Bass

When bass just aren't biting, rig a 4-inch plastic worm on a 1/16 or 1/8 oz. leadhead and leave the hook point exposed. Cast the worm to rocky banks, let it sink a few feet, keep the rod tip at the 10 o'clock position, then start reeling the worm back to the boat slowly and methodically without moving the rod. This "do nothing" retrieve will trick bass on the worst fishing days.

Use Streamlined Lures In Current

Lures such as jigs, metal spoons, tailspinners and blade baits are ideal for use in river current. These streamlined baits are subject to less current drag than bulkier baits, enabling them to be presented more accurately in moving water.

Target Midstream Cover

Bass inhabiting rivers and streams often hold around submerged cover located well off the banks. Fish hiding in a submerged tree or rockpile in the middle of the stream can take advantage of prey approaching from a much wider area than bass holding against a current-breaking object close to shore.

The Fleeing-Baitfish Retrieve

In murky water, try retrieving a large spinnerbait with a Colorado blade quickly so it runs just beneath the surface. The rotating blade will create a wake that resembles the one made by a fleeing baitfish. If this fails to produce, slow your retrieve and make repeated casts to the same area, giving the bass ample time to locate your offering.

A Simple Rule For Retrieving Spinnerbaits

How fast should you retrieve a spinnerbait? A simple rule is to retrieve the lure at the speed at which you can barely see its blades flashing. If you follow this formula, the retrieve will be slower in clear water so the lure runs deeper. In murky water, the retrieve will be faster so the lure runs closer to the surface.

Wear Polarized Sunglasses

Viewers of my tv show occasionally write in to ask why I'm always wearing sunglasses when I'm fishing, even on cloudy days. No, it's not because I'm trying to look cool—Polarized sunglasses greatly reduce the glare reflecting off the water's surface, allowing the angler to see fish-holding objects such as rocks, stumps and logs (as well as the fish themselves) more clearly. Keep at least two pairs of glare-reducing sunglasses handy when you're fishing — one with gray lenses for sunny conditions, and another with brown or yellow lenses for overcast conditions.

Bill's trademark sunglasses help him spot fish-holding objects. This 7 1/2 lb. smallmouth bass was holding next to a submerged rock.

Cold Front Tactics

When a cold front passes through, bass often go into a holding pattern until weather conditions improve. In lakes without much shallow cover, move to the first significant depth change and fish a jig or plastic worm slowly on the bottom. In lakes with plenty of shallow logs, stumps or weeds, fish in the thickest tangles with these same lures.

Rough Spot

Smallmouth and spotted bass have a rough patch on the floor of their mouths, which biologists believe they use to help them hold onto crayfish more securely.

Vertical Structure

Spotted bass show a marked propensity for vertical structure, such as steep rock bluffs or trees standing in deep water. They'll often suspend around this structure, sometimes at extreme depths, and can be caught by jigging a spoon.

Look For Bait

Not sure where to fish? Look for bait—chances are bass will be somewhere close by. Bass are opportunists and will seldom be far from a source of food. In shallow water, look for minnows flipping on the surface. In deep water, use your boat's graph to locate suspended clouds of baitfish.

Short-Line Strategies

Pitching and flipping are two short-line casting techniques that are ideal when bass are holding tight to submerged cover. They allow the angler to make many short presentations to "saturate" a small area with a weedless lure such as a plastic worm or jig 'n' pig, and are most effective during cold fronts or any time the bass bite is slow. They require the use of a long (6 1/2-7 ft.), medium-heavy to heavy-action baitcasting rod and stout line testing 20 to 30 lbs.

A Trick For Surfacing Bass

If schooling bass are changing locations quickly, a metal spoon is your best lure choice. You can cast a spoon much farther than a wood or plastic surface lure, enabling you to reach surfacing bass from a greater distance. As soon as the spoon hits the water, hold your rod high and reel quickly so the lure darts and skitters across the surface like a panic-stricken baitfish.

Keep It Moving

When retrieving a weedless lure across the top of lilypads or pond scum, keep it moving at a fairly slow, constant pace. This gives the bass plenty of opportunity to track down the lure. Avoid using a stop-and-go retrieve, for the bass may strike at the lure and miss it.

Shake It

Shaking is a technique perfected by Western anglers that works anywhere bass swim. Cast a plastic worm, grub or jig and let it sink all the way to the bottom. Reel up slack very slowly until you can feel the lure's weight. Then hold the rod tip at the 10 o'clock position and shake it very gently, so the lure's tail or skirt wriggles while the head remains on the bottom. This tactic works best in clear lakes with a rocky bottom.

Are Big Bass Always Deep?

Bass fishermen often believe the biggest bass in the lake stay deep, but in most natural lakes, the biggest largemouths may actually live surprisingly shallow, providing there's plenty of shallow cover available. A survey of Florida anglers who had caught verified largemouths weighing over 15 lbs. apiece indicated that nearly 90% of these giant bass came from 3 feet of water or less.

Scents Make Sense

A fish-attracting lure scent can greatly enhance your fishing success. Using scent on your lures is especially beneficial in murky water, when bass rely greatly on senses other than sight; when fishing highly-pressured water, when bass are shy to bite; and during a cold front, when bass are sluggish and often short-strike a lure. Douse your lure liberally with attractant—bass will bite it more readily and hang onto it much longer.

How To Rig A Live Crayfish

A live crayfish is one of the most effective baits for lunker bass. Use a small rubber band to lash a light wire hook to the craw's tail, then fish it unweighted on light line across points and gravel bars.

Heavyweight Bass

Most fishermen believe bass are heaviest in early spring, when they're carrying eggs. But in reality, bass tend to be heaviest in mid to late summer, when they gorge themselves on baitfish to satisfy their increased metabolic activity.

Binge Feeders

Summer bass are binge feeders. Rather than risk stressing themselves by expending a great deal of energy hunting food in hot water, they hold around cover on points, ledges and other offshore structures for extended periods, then feed heavily on passing baitfish when the opportunity presents itself.

Gravy Train

Sometimes a seemingly-insignificant bit of cover can greatly enhance the appeal of a large piece of structure to bass. Bass pros know that a patch of weeds on the end of a deep point, or a single stump on top of a submerged hump, can be the "gravy" it takes to make a good bassin' spot even better.

Rust Never Sleeps

Many soft plastic lures contain salt. Avoid storing hooks alongside these baits—the salt will corrode them.

Catch & Release

Releasing the bass you catch today will help ensure good fishing tomorrow. Use a camera to record the memory of your catch, then slide the fish gently into the water. It'll be even bigger next season.

Balancing Act

How fast or slow a jig falls is one of the most important factors determining how bass will react to it. You can control the speed at which your jig drops in three ways: (1) use a jig with a lighter or heavier head, (2) add a larger or smaller trailer to the lure, or (3) snip off some of the skirt to thin it out.

Poppin' Bass

When bass are hiding in weedbeds growing beneath the surface, try a surface popper. This noisy lure will antagonize bass into striking when popped repeatedly over their heads.

Peg It

A Texas-rigged worm is deadly around weedbeds and sunken brushpiles. To increase the efficiency of this presentation, "peg" the sliding sinker by inserting a small piece of toothpick into the hole. This will prevent the weight from sliding on the line, thereby making it easier for the lure to crawl through heavy cover without hanging up.

Vary Leader Lengths

Vary the length of the leader used on your Carolina worm rig to meet fishing conditions. When using the rig on weedy bottoms, use a long (4-5 ft.) leader so the worm suspends above the vegetation. When fishing rocky areas, use a shorter (2-4 ft.) leader so the lure remains closer to the bottom.

Increase Your Trailer's Action

To enhance the action of a pork or soft plastic trailer on a jig or spinnerbait, cut several shallow notches in the underside of the trailer body and legs with a sharp knife. This will increase the trailer's flexibility and give it a more sinuous swimming action.

Try Hot Colors

Can't buy a strike? Try a spinnerbait or jig in a hot color such as blaze orange or chatreuse. These outrageous hues don't look like anything in nature, but they can provoke a reaction strike from a moody bass.

Match The Hatch

Stream trout fishermen know it pays to "hatch the hatch" by using flies that resemble hatching insects. Bass fishermen can use this same approach with their jigs and crankbaits. The crayfish that these lures mimic vary in size and color from one season or body of water to the next. Before fishing, turn over rocks at the water's edge and examine the crayfish hiding there. Then use lures that match the size and color of these bass delicacies.

Bass Saunas

In winter, an underground spring entering a lake or river can be a veritable hotspot for bass. Spring water will be considerably warmer than surrounding lake or river water and can pull in both baitfish and bass in droves. Since spring water is usually extremely clear, use small lures and light line for a more realistic presentation.

Get Your Spoon Back

Replace your jigging spoon's steel hook with a softer bronze hook, and use heavy line. If you hang up the spoon in a deep treetop, move directly over the obstruction, jiggle the rod tip and the lure will usually pop free. If it doesn't, tighten the reel drag and pull until you straighten the hook.

Why Bass Use Shade

Many fishermen believe bass lurk in shady places because the sun hurts their eyes. Wrong! The bass is a member of the sunfish family, and can often be seen basking in direct sunlight along the shallow margins of lakes and rivers. But when they're serious about feeding, bass, like most predators, use shade to conceal themselves from their prey.

Big Surface Lures At Night

Nothing is more thrilling than the sound of a lunker bass smashing a surface lure at night. Cast a big, dark-colored topwater wobbler, popper, prop bait or buzz bait close to weedlines or shallow shorelines after dark. Use heavy line, and don't set the hook before feeling the fish pull.

A Smallmouth Tip For Cold Water

When the temperature of the lake drops below 45 degrees, smallmouth bass often suspend off points and rock bluffs and become hard to catch with traditional lures and methods. These fish can be taken on a tiny crappie jig or grub fished beneath a slip bobber. Using a long, light-action spinning rod, rig a 1/16 oz. jig on 4 lb. line and attach the slip bobber above the jig, adjusting the bobber to present the lure 3 to 12 ft. deep, depending on where the fish are holding. Cast and allow the wave action to subtly activate the jig by moving the bobber. When the float goes under, set the hook—a smallmouth has inhaled the jig.

Use The Reel Handle

If bass aren't responding to your bottom-bumping presentation with a jig or worm, maybe it's because you're trying to impart too much action to the lure via your rod tip. Instead of jerking the rod repeatedly so the lure hops actively, try holding the rod steady at the 10 o'clock position and using only the reel handle to move the lure. If the bait hangs up momentarily behind a rock or other bottom object, tighten down on the line with the reel handle and gently flip the rod tip—the lure will resemble a darting crayfish or minnow when it pops free.

Play Big Bass Carefully

Hooking a big bass is one of fishing's most exciting moments. To make sure you get the fish in the boat, play it carefully. Try to keep the bass a good distance from the boat during the initial stages of the fight—a "green" bass on a short length of line is an invitation to trouble. <u>If the fish wants to jump, keep the rod tip close to the water to minimize slack line.</u>

Isolated Objects Attract Bass

Bass are drawn to isolated objects—a lone stump on the end of a point, a small patch of grass growing a couple of boat-lengths from a large weedbed, etc. Target this randomly-scattered cover first—often that's where the biggest bass in the area will be.

Scoring In High, Muddy Rivers

High, muddy water doesn't have to turn your next river fishing trip into a disaster. Cast jigs, crankbaits and other bottom-bumping lures right next to the bank. The shoreline's irregular features will greatly diminish the current's velocity so bass can hold there comfortably. But make sure your lures graze the shoreline, because bass in muddy water won't move far to strike. If possible, make several casts to the same location, always casting upstream and retrieving your lure with the current for a lifelike presentation.

Bass Love Bluegills

Bass frequently dine on small bluegills, especially in weedy lakes and ponds. Use a dark green or brown diving crankbait with an orange belly to mimic a bite-sized bluegill.

Low-Water Lesson

Once a reservoir has been drawn down for the winter, many structural elements that are beneath the surface during the fishing season may be revealed to the naked eye. Cruise the lake, notin the location of stumps, rockpiles, ditches, channels and other normally-hidden features on a topographic map. You can also photograph or videotape the lake during drawdown as a permanent visual reference.

How To Sting A Bass

Bass often short-strike a spinnerbait or buzz bait. Adding a stinger hook to these lures will greatly increase your percentage of hookups. If <u>the terrain will permit, reversing the hook so the</u> <u>point rides down will work even better.</u>

Stingers On Soft Jerk Baits

A stinger hook works great on a soft plastic jerk bait, too. After running a worm hook through the head of the bait, pass the end of the hook through the eye of a small treble hook, then complete the rigging of the worm hook as you usually would. The treble stinger will even hook bass that make a pass at the lure without actually biting it.

Weedless Pork

A fat pork frog or eel is one of the deadliest lures you can use for big bass in heavy weeds. Simply rig it weightless on a stout weedless hook and cast it into the grassbed—it will slide and slither over and through the thickest vegetation.

A pork eel rigged on a weedless hook can slither through the thick cover where big largemouths lurk.

Migration Routes

Bass use "migration routes" when moving from deep to shallow water in spring, and from shallow to deep water in fall. They'll swim along creek channels, long points, ditches, stump rows and other structures, occasionally stopping to hold around objects they encounter along the way. Use your depth finder and a topo map of the lake to locate these bass highways.

Falling-Water Strategy

When the lake or river's level is falling, bass will pull off the banks and away from shallow cover to head for deeper water. Many bass will hold along the first rapid depth change out from the bank, such as a ledge or channel dropoff, until conditions stabilize and the lake level returns to normal.

Fantastic Flats

Flats are often-overlooked structures that can hold big large-mouth bass in spring through fall. Largemouths will be attracted to any irregular features (depressions, ditches, ridges, etc.) as well as stumps, downed trees and brushpiles scattered along the expanse of the flat. If the water is murky, flip a jig or worm around this cover; if it's clear or slightly stained, try a spinnerbait or lipless crankbait.

Spring Smallmouth Flats

In spring, smallmouth bass will spawn on patches of gravel located on mud or clay flats adjacent to deep water. Locate these smallmouth magnets during winter drawdown, especially in short creek arms and coves.

Flat Crankbaits In Cold Water

A flat-sided crankbait is a great choice in cold water. These lures don't vibrate as hard as a rounded crankbait, making them better suited to sluggish bass. In early spring, many bass pros fish 'em around shallow logs and stumps, the same places you'd normally fish a spinnerbait.

Rip It

In cold water, try ripping a suspending jerk bait. Cast, reel the lure down a few feet, then jerk the rod tip sharply so the bait makes a short, frantic run like a fleeing baitfish. Pause, reel up slack line and repeat.

Lunar Logic

<u>Insects time their hatches around the new or full moon</u>. This is an effective survival strategy—when billions of bugs hatch out at the same time, it's impossible for predators to eat them all, so the survival of the species is assured. <u>Bass are attuned to feeding heavily during these prime lunar periods</u>—no wonder many anglers report excellent fishing during the new and full moon.

Parallel The Bank

When fishing a sharply-vertical structure such as a rock bluff or a grassline with a diving crankbait, position your boat so you can retrieve the lure parallel to the bank. This will keep it near the edge of the cover, in the strike zone, during the entire retrieve. If you put your boat in deep water and cast into the structure, the lure will be in open water for the majority of the retrieve, and your chances of a strike will decline greatly.

Silent Approach

Roaring into the area you want to fish with your outboard motor will put bass on red alert. Instead, turn off your outboard at least four castlengths from your fishing spot, then either drift into casting position with the wind or use your electric trolling motor to move you closer.

Two-Tone Trailers

To enhance the visibility of your spinnerbait or jig presentation without resorting to a totally bright-colored lure which bass might be reluctant to strike, try a two-tone trailer, such as a black/chartreuse or brown/orange pork frog. This will give the lure a subtle shot of color that often draws a quick response from bass.

A Spinnerbait Tactic For Smallmouths

In clear, rocky lakes, smallmouths often suspend in open water off main-lake structures such as rockpiles and points. Cast a spinnerbait with bright chartreuse blades and retrieve it quickly so it runs a foot or so under the surface. Bass can see this hot-colored lure from great distances; this tactic has been known to pull entire schools of smallmouths out of deep water to the surface.

A New Fishin' Hole

When weeds choke the lake in summer, use a rake to make fishing holes in the vegetation. Rake out an opening in the grass, then return in a day or two to fish the hole—bass will gravitate to the newly-created edge.

Don't Jerk Out The Hook

Bass are often lightly-hooked on crankbaits, so when you feel a bass strike, don't jerk back the rod sharply to set the hook. Instead, sweep the rod low and to one side, or simply turn the reel handle rapidly to tighten down on the fish—with today's super-sharp treble hooks, this is often enough to bury the barb.

Terrific Tubes

Tube baits are great for big bass in clear water. Fish them around sunken rocks, boulders and brushpiles on light line with a fast-action spinning rod and a strong, light-wire hook.

Carolina Tubes

To cover a lot of water quickly with a tube bait, fish it on a Carolina rig. Fill the hollow tube with Styrofoam packing material to make it float, then rig it with a light wire hook on a leader. A dose of fish attractant inside the tube can further enhance its bass appeal.

A New Twist On Spoons

A metal jigging spoon can easily twist your line, but the savvy angler can use this to his advantage. After jigging the spoon repeatedly on deep structure, hold your rod still for a few seconds so the line untwists—the spoon will spin rapidly in place, which can result in a sudden strike.

Don't Send Metal Lures Into Orbit

Never tie monofilament line directly to a metal lure like a jigging spoon or blade bait. The sharp metal on the edge of the tie hole will eventually cut the line, meaning you may put the lure "into orbit" on your next cast. Use a split ring, wire snap or snap swivel to attach your line to a metal lure.

Crank Submerged Roadbeds

Examine a topo map of your local reservoir to locate roads that may have been inundated when the lake was formed. Submerged roadbeds are often lined with stumps, gravel and brushpiles, making them great habitat for bass. Use a deep-diving crankbait to get to the bottom of these bass structures.

Root Deep-Divers Shallow

Sometimes a deep-diving crankbait is your best bet in shallow water. If the bottom isn't too weedy, you can root a crankbait with a long diving lip through the shallows; as it moves, it will kick up clouds of silt and skitter across the bottom erratically, looking much like a live crayfish to a hungry bass.

A Wishy-Washy Retrieve

On a windy day, cast a floater/diver minnow lure onto a point or steep bank being pounded by waves. Leave some slack in the line and let the waves wash the lure back and forth for several seconds. Often a bass will swim up and grab the lure, mistaking it for an injured baitfish floundering helplessly in the waves.

Shake In The Grass

Sometimes weedbeds are so thick and matted on the surface, they seem impossible to penetrate. Pitch a heavy jig 'n' pig onto the mat and shake the rod tip repeatedly; eventually the lure will work its way through the mat to bass waiting in the open water below.

Boat Dock Savvy

Bass often hide beneath boat docks, where they find plenty of shade to conceal themselves. But not all docks are created equal. The best docks are usually located along banks that either have plenty of shallow grass or have been dredged out to form a deep trench, or those built closer to deeper water.

Brushpiles And Docks

When fishing a boat dock, don't just target your lures to the dock itself—fish in front of the dock as well. Dock owners hoping to attract crappie often sink old Christmas trees and brush here if the water is deep enough. Night lights on the dock are a good tipoff that cover is present.

Clip The Bottom Hook

If your crankbait keeps hanging up in brushy areas, use wire cutters to clip the bottom hook from the treble hanging form the bait's belly. This is usually the lowest-running hook on the lure; clipping it off shouldn't adversely affect the lure's bass-catching capability.

The Slack-Line Hookset

When you feel a bass bite your worm or jig, immediately lower the rod tip and bring it back sharply, so you snap the slack out of the line. This hookset will drive the point through the tough jaw of a bass in much the same way that the blow of a hammer drives a nail through a board.

Crawl It In

When fishing a pond or natural lake, try casting a weedless lure such as a jig, plastic worm or plastic frog right up onto the bank and crawling or hopping it into the water. This is a highly realistic presentation wherever bass hold in shallow weeds growing out from the shoreline, and gives the lure the appearance of a live frog or other small terrestrial creature.

Surface Lures In Streams

Be sure to try surface lures when wading streams. Bass living in narrow creeks become attuned to feeding on small reptiles, mammals and insects swimming from one bank to another, and will readily strike a small topwater offering such as a quarter-ounce prop bait.

The Most Realistic Lures

Big bass don't get that way by biting the first thing that swims along. Over time, they learn to avoid danger by feeding on creatures they can safely swallow, such as shiners and shad. These abundant forage fish have soft rays in their fins that collapse easily and won't stick in the throat. Bass recognize the long, slender profile and metallic flash of these baitfish as positive cues when feeding. Therefore it makes sense to use artificial lures that present similar cues, especially when the water is clear and bass may scrutinize your lures carefully before striking. No wonder long, slender floater/diver minnows in shiny chrome, silver or gold color patterns and plastic worms in light-catching flake colors are so deadly on big bass.

Try Flat Finishes On Cloudy Days

If it's overcast or raining, lures in flat finishes often far outfish reflective colors. A reflective finish loses its fish-attracting flash when sunlight is diminished, and mirrors the grayness of the sky and water around it, making it hard for the bass to see. Black and bone white are good color options on dark days.

Use Prop Baits In Choppy Water

In choppy water above 65 degrees, try fishing a noisy prop bait on the surface. Fishing the lure with a rip/pause/rip retrieve will create considerable surface commotion which bass will mistake for a floundering baitfish.

Use Bite-Sized Lures In Cold Water

It takes bass considerably longer to digest a meal in cold water than in warm water. Therefore bass in cold water don't feed often, and tend to take smaller bites when they do feed. This explains why a compact lure like a 1/8 oz. jig is a far better bet for bass in cold conditions than a large lure like a 3/4 oz. crankbait or 9-in. plastic worm.

Make Your Own Livewell

A old insulated cooler can be used to make an excellent livewell for a small boat. Attach an aerator pump or aquarium bubbler to the inside of the tank to oxygenate the water; these pumps draw little current when powered by a small 12-volt battery.

Fish 45-Degree Banks In Winter

Banks with a sharp (at least 45-degree) slope into deep water are the most predictable places to locate bass during the winter months. Bass can go from deep to shallow water on these sloping banks without moving a long distance. They often have numerous outcroppings (ledges) and indentations (cuts) along their slope which provide good places for crayfish to hide and for bass to hold. Fish 'em with a slow-sinking leadhead lure such as a grub or hair jig.

Mark Your Line

Keep a waterproof marker handy when vertical-jigging for suspended fish. When you hook a fish, immediately mark the line just below the rod tip. This will indicate exactly how deep the fish was hooked and will allow you to easily return to that depth the next time you lower your spoon.

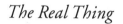

The Real Thing

All artificial lures are a simulation of reality, but live bait is the real thing. It moves, looks and acts real because it *is* real, and is therefore totally convincing to even the most wary bass. No wonder most of the biggest bass taken annually are caught on live bait.

Fish Shiners In Overhead Cover

In summer, dense fields of hyacinths, milfoil, hydrilla, lilypads, or spatterdock can cover wide expanses of many lakes and rivers. Big bass love to hold beneath this overhead cover, but it can be intimidating to fish. One way to successfully attack it is with a wild shiner. Anchor the boat at both ends to keep it from drifting in the wind or current. Hook a large, lively shiner just above its vent with a stout weedless hook, drop it into the water, and let it swim freely. It will usually head straight for the vegetation and, with occasional gentle tugs with the rod tip to coax it along, will eventually swim far beneath the cover—and right into the jaws of a lunker bass.

Even though there was snow on the ground and the water was frigid, this hawg put up quite a fight.

Bluegills are ideal for introducing kids to the fun of fishing.

PANFISH
Interesting Facts About America's Family-Fun Fish

Bluegill

Members of this large fish family include bluegills, shellcrackers and sunfish. All are short, rounded in shape and pugnacious predators. Some form of these feisty gamefish can be caught in nearly every lake, reservoir, pond and river across North America. Bluegills have a rounded profile and are often brightly colored. They prefer shallow water and typically occur in large numbers along the margins of ponds and lakes. They're best caught on live baits, especially worms and crickets, and on small artificial lures. The largest bluegill ever recorded came from Ketona Lake, Ala. and weighed 4 lb. 12 oz.

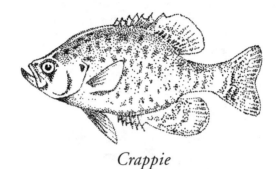

Crappie

These popular panfish are favored by anglers for their tasty flesh. They're abundant in waters across America. Two main varieties, the white and black crappie, reside in North American waters. Crappie are attracted to submerged wood and vegetation and usually suspend above the bottom; they can occur in large schools, especially during the spawning season. Anglers catch crappie on live bait (especially small minnow) as well as artificial lures. The official world record black crappie (4 lb. 8 oz.) was caught in Kerr Lake, Va.; this species has been reported up to 6 lbs. The world record white crappie, from Enid Lake, Miss., weighed 5 lb. 3 oz.

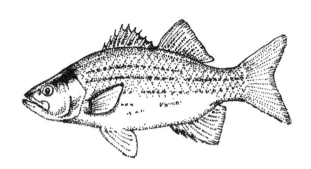

White Bass

This striped fighter thrives in rivers and lakes in much of the U. S. It travels in large schools across open water and will occasionally chase baitfish such as threadfin shad to the surface when feeding. The white bass is at home in current and makes an annual spawning run into the headwaters of river systems. Anglers catch it on a variety of artificial lures as well as live minnows. The world record white bass, 6 lb. 13 oz., came from Lake Orange, Va.

PANFISHING TIPS

How To Keep Bait Lively

Panfish experts agree that fresh, lively bait is vital for panfishing success. Keep minnows cool and well-aerated in your boat's livewell or in a bucket with an aerator pump. Night crawlers should be kept cool and moist in a container packed with worm bedding or moss. Crickets should be kept out of direct sunlight in a screened container; they'll stay hoppin' fresh if you feed them some moist bread scraps between fishing trips.

Slabs Love Big Stumps

The biggest crappie often hang out close to large stumps near deep water. While you'll probably catch greater numbers of these fish around brush or smaller stumps, if you're after a real "slab," target big stumps with live minnows and small jigs.

Use Lightweight Jigs

Small soft-plastic jigs are tremendous lures for all species of panfish, but don't use one that's too heavy. Start with a light (1/32 to 1/16 oz.) leadhead—this will have a slow, enticing fall, just like an injured minnow. White, pink and chartreuse are proven colors. Cast them around shallow wood cover and swim them back to the boat with a slow, steady retrieve. If fish happen to be deep, or if the wind picks up, switch to a heavier jig. Store panfish jigs in a multi-sectioned clear plastic utility box and write their weight on the lid above each section with a waterproof marker.

Hunt Irregular Features

Shallow crappie are seldom right up against the bank. Rather, they gravitate to irregular features such as ditches, channels, high spots or isolated patches of cover that occur on large structural elements such as mud flats or shallow points. Locate these subtle hotspots with your depth finder and you'll strike crappie gold.

Fish Vertically In Cover

Crappie and bluegill often gather in giant schools around submerged brushpiles. The most efficient way to probe these snaggy structures is to drop a jig or live minnow straight down below your boat. Use a long crappie pole or flyrod to s-l-o-w-l-y lower the bait or lure into or alongside of the cover—often it'll "get bit" before it reaches the bottom.

Twist-Tails Rule

Arguably the most productive (and least expensive) artificial lure for all panfish varieties is the soft plastic twist-tail grub.

I caught this slab crappie by vertical-fishing a tiny jig around standing timber in a Mississippi lake.

Two-inch grubs work great for crappie and bluegill; white bass often favor 3- and 4-inchers. Bright colors usually produce the best results, but experiment to find which colors work best in your home waters. Buy grubs and leadheads in economical bulk bags.

Heavy Metal

Many Southeastern crappie fishermen favor the "Kentucky rig," which features a heavy (1/2 to 1 oz.) bell sinker on the end of a line to which two short leaders made of stiff monofiliment catfish line are attached. The sinker is dropped straight down into a submerged tree or brushpile and gently raised and lowered until fish are contacted. The stiff mono leaders stand straight out from the main line for a tangle-free bait or lure presentation.

Create Your Own Cover

Where legal, serious crappie fishermen sink their own crappie cover. Sinking stake beds, brushpiles or old Christmas trees at varying depths around the lake will take shifting water levels and changing crappie moods into account.

Bite-Sized Baits

Worms are a good bait for bluegills—so good, in fact, that you'll go through scores of worms in no time unless you economize. Once you've attracted a large school of 'gills to your fishing area, use progressively smaller bits of worm on your hook—these panfish are competitive, and when there's a school present, they'll readily bite even the tiniest chunk of worm the instant it hits the water.

A Trolling Trick For Big White Bass

When white bass school, the biggest fish often hang out below the rest of the pack, where they pick off dead and injured baitfish their smaller cousins may have missed. Get down to their level by attaching a white hair jig or twist-tail grub to the trailing hook of a deep-diving crankbait via a 2-ft. leader line. For best results, troll this rig in open water.

It's Yucky, But It Works

One of the best live baits for slab crappie and bull bluegill is a catalpa worm, a greenish caterpillar that eats the leaves of the catalpa tree. This critter has a leathery hide that makes it nearly impossible for panfish to steal from your hook. Okay, now here's the bad news: the time-honored method of rigging this worm is to turn it inside-out with a stick or nail before impaling it on your hook.

One of the biggest catfish ever caught on rod and reel, this 112 lb. blue came from the Cumberland River, Tenn.

CATFISH
Things You Should Know About These
Tasty Fighters

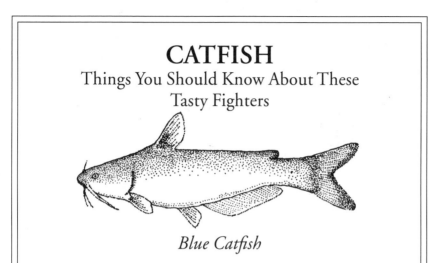

Blue Catfish

These freshwater monsters can attain a weight of over 100 lbs. and represent an exciting challenge for the serious angler. Primarily fish-eaters, blues love deep water and can commonly be encountered in reservoirs and rivers on channel structure at depths of 40 to 60 feet. Blue cats are native to America's major river systems and have been widely introduced elsewhere across the nation. The world record blue cat was caught from the Cumberland River, Tenn., and weighed 112 lbs.

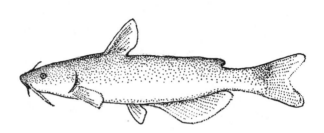

Channel Catfish

The channel catfish is one of America's favorite family fish—abundant, easy to catch and great table fare. It's our most common catfish species and can be found in lakes, rivers, streams and reservoirs virtually everywhere across the nation. Channel cats favor warmer and shallower water than blues and can be caught on a wide variety of prepared baits as well as night crawlers, minnows and liver. The world record channel cat, from Santee-Cooper Reservoir, S. C., weighed 58 lbs.

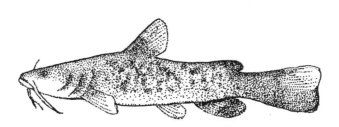

Flathead Catfish

The flathead favors murky reservoirs and slow-moving rivers, where it spends much of the day holed up in rock rubble and submerged trees. At night, it emerges from hiding to prowl shallow creek arms and bays for its favorite prey, large shad, bluegills and rough fish. It's extremely well-camouflaged to muddy bottoms and will gulp down just about anything that wanders too close to its massive jaws. A big flathead is one of our hardest-fighting gamefish—just wait 'til you hook one and that club-like tail swings into action! The world record flathead was caught in Toledo Bend Reservoir, Tex. and weighed 92 lbs.

CATFISHING TIPS

Sensory Overload

The catfish is one giant sensory organ. Taste buds cover its entire body, and it has a highly-developed sense of smell. Little wonder prepared "stink baits" are so effective on cats!

This huge catfish was taken on prepared bait fished on a jugline—a deadly tactic in river current.

99

Big Blues Love Cold Water

The biggest blue catfish often come from water below the 40-degree mark. Most other gamefish are sluggish in water this frigid, but not blues—they'll bite aggressively and put up a world-class fight.

Flatheads On Bluegills

One of the best baits for a big flathead catfish is a live bluegill. Fish it under a float in shallow water, or below a heavy sinker on the bottom of a river. Use stout tackle—when hooked, a flathead usually heads straight for cover.

Juggin' Fun

One of the easiest and most enjoyable ways to catch catfish is on juglines. Wrap a length of strong monofiliment line around the neck of a plastic milk jug. Pull out the desired length (6 to 10 ft. is usually plenty) and secure the remainder in place with a sturdy rubber band. Rig a stout live bait hook at the end of the line and a heavy sinker (an old spark plug or wheel weight will work) about a foot above the hook. Use liver, worms, minnows, shrimp or prepared catfish bait. Put out several jugs away from heavy boating traffic, then get set for fun as catfish try to make off with them. Always check local regulations before jug fishing.

Cats On Corks

In spring, catfish often move around shallow rock banks to spawn. They can be caught using live minnows or prepared baits drifted shallow beneath slip bobbers.

The Three-Way Rig

The three-way rig is a great live bait setup for catfish in current, and with some variation of the leader length, sinker size and/or bait used, will work well for stripers, walleye and other moving-water species, too. Attach a three-way swivel to the tag end of your main line. Tie a short length of lighter-weight line to the bottom swivel ring and attach a pyramid sinker to the end. Then tie a longer (24-36 in.) section of line to the remaining ring (this leader should test the same as your main line) with a bait hook at the end. Rig with live bait, cut pieces of fish, liver or prepared bait and let sit on the bottom in current.

Catfish Attractor

A "fish block" is a great catfish attractor. These biodegradable blocks, when submerged, emit a fish-attracting odor which will call catfish and baitfish from a wide area. Tie a block to a tree limb or boat dock to attract fish close to shore, or sink one or more on underwater structure. For best results, return in a couple of days and fish close to the block.

OTHER POPULAR GAMEFISH

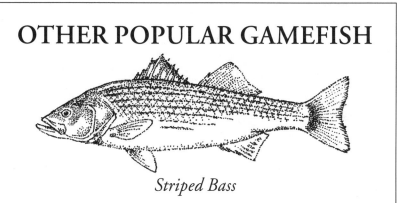

Striped Bass

One of the largest North American gamefish, the striper is a hard-hitting, hard-pulling heavyweight. Although it's a true saltwater species, it has been successfully stocked across the nation in freshwater rivers and reservoirs with cool, well-oxygenated water and an abundant supply of forage fish such as shad or herring. It often travels in large schools and will attack both live baits and artificial lures. Stripers are most active at dawn and dusk and usually suspend or hold around submerged timber during mid-day. The world record striper from fresh water came from O'Neill Forebay, Cal. and weighed 67 lb. 8 oz.

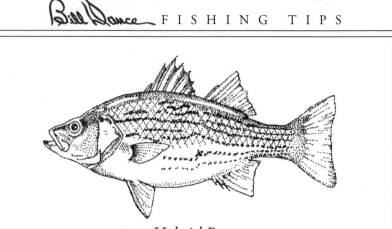

Hybrid Bass

Also known as the whiterock or wiper, this exciting gamefish is a cross of the female striped bass and the male white bass. It resembles a striper but is shorter and stockier, and has broken stripes. Hybrids can tolerate warmer water than stripers and have been heavily stocked in recent years in many reservoirs. They primarily eat shad and other open-water baitfish and, like stripers, will wander the lake in large wolfpacks following bait-fish schools. The world record hybrid is a 25 lb. 8 oz. specimen from Chatuge Lake, Ga.

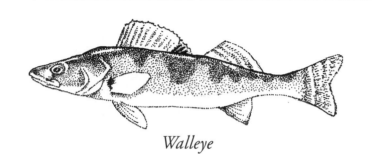

Walleye

"Ol' Marble-Eyes" is a toothy predator that's most active at dusk. Most popular in the northern United States, the walleye's popularity is growing steadily since it has been successfully stocked in reservoirs and rivers as far south as Alabama and as far west as Washington. Although it lacks the striper's pulling power or the smallmouth basses' jumping ability, the walleye is one of the most challenging of all gamefish to catch and is widely regarded as one of the finest-eating fish that swims. This highly-adaptable species is at home in rocky rivers, sprawling reservoirs and grassy, natural lakes. Its smaller cousin, the sauger, is often abundant in the fast water below dams. The world record walleye was caught in Greers Ferry Lake, Ark. and weighed 22 lb. 11 oz.

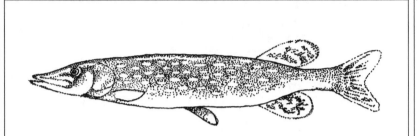

Northern Pike

One of our most adaptable gamefish, the northern pike thrives in weedy lakes, deep reservoirs and slow-moving rivers. It favors 50 to 55 degree water, but can tolerate much colder conditions—this fish occurs in lakes as far north as the Arctic Circle. It is well-camouflaged to aquatic weedbeds, which it prowls in search of suckers, bluegills and other fish. The world record northern pike, 55 lb. 1 oz., came from Lake of Grefeern, West Germany.

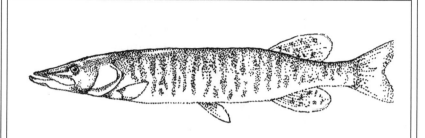

Musky

"The fish of 10,000 casts" is arguably our most challenging gamefish—it's temperamental to the extreme. A close relative of the northern pike, the musky (short for *muskellunge*) has a more limited range and prefers slightly warmer water. It favors aquatic weedbeds in lakes, rivers and reservoirs, and will attack rough fish, ducks, small mammals, even boat propellers. The world record musky, from Chippewa Flowage, Wis., weighed 69 lb. 11 oz.

STRIPER & HYBRID TIPS

Fish Above The Fish

When they're suspended, stripers and hybrids are notorious for refusing to swim downward to feed. After using your graph or flasher to determine the depth at which these gamefish are suspending, measure out enough line so your baited hook is just above the level of the fish.

Be An Early Bird

I've never been one to be on the water before the crack of dawn, but I make an effort to get going extra-early when I'm fishing for stripers or hybrids. These fish are low-light feeders and are usually most active around daybreak. Topwater lures are a great choice now—don't be surprised if a monster slams your surface bait on the very first cast!

Keep Tabs On Temperature

Stripers show a marked preference for cool water. They'll be most active in water between approximately 52 and 65 degrees, so focus your fishing efforts on places within this preferred range. To find it, take frequent readings using your boat's surface temperature gauge or use a pool thermometer.

Rivers For Giants

Some of the biggest stripers and hybrids live in rivers. Moving water is high in dissolved oxygen and cooler than still water in summer, warmer in winter. These eating machine need plenty of groceries, and rivers contain tremendous quantities of baitfish. Stripers and hybrids usually occur shallower in rivers than they do in slackwater reservoirs, making them easier to locate and catch, especially on topwater lures and other artificials. Best of all, rivers are much less highly-pressured than lakes, which means they're often loaded with big fish.

Stripers are low-light feeders. Co-author Don Wirth caught this 46-pounder on his first cast at daybreak.

Use A Shad Tank

Experienced striper and hybrid anglers use a shad tank to keep these baitfish frisky. This specially-designed tank has rounded interior walls which help prevent delicate shad from running into the corners and damaging themselves, plus a circular aeration system which gently pumps oxygen into the water without knocking scales off your bait. Shad tanks are available at bait shops and through mail order catalogs, or you can make your own from an empty plastic drum.

Tiny Temptations

When the water temperature drops below 50 degrees in winter, think small for big stripers. These gamefish often prefer smaller food portions during the winter than in other seasons. Some real giants have been taken by live bait anglers substituting their usual large shad or herring for tiny crappie minnows. Lure fishermen should downsize their offerings as well—now is a great time to try a small hair jig or leadhead grub.

Sometimes it takes a small bait to catch a big striper. Priest Lake, Tennessee, guide Jack Christian caught this 35-pounder from 45-degree water on a 2-inch crappie minnow.

Target Submerged Wood

Stripers are often thought of as being an open-water gamefish, and this is usually true in a deep reservoir. But in a shallow river, they'll hang out around sunken trees, stumps and other wood cover—just like largemouth bass in a lake. This is most likely to occur during the middle of the day, when stripers aren't actively cruising for a meal. Make sure to fish your lures and live baits close to wood once the sun gets high.

Alternative Baits For Hybrids

Most hybrid anglers drift live shad and shiners to catch these hard-pulling gamefish, but they'll take other baits as well. Fishermen nationwide report good success catching hybrids off the bottom on chicken livers, live and dead crayfish and dead shad, either whole or cut into pieces. Studies by fisheries biologists have confirmed that hybrids often scour the bottom for a quick meal. Bottom-fishing works especially well for hybrids in tailraces below dams.

WALLEYE TIPS

Use Slender Plugs

Slender crankbaits and minnow imitators are often your best choice for walleye. Cast or troll them around suspended bait-fish schools in open water, and across shallow gravel bars in rivers.

Tip Jigs With Bait

Walleye pros report heavy catches on small jigs tipped with live minnows or leeches. These can be drifted in open water, cast and retrieved around weedy flats or bounced along rocky river bottoms.

Slender crankbaits with long diving lips are perfect bottom-bouncing lures for big walleye.

The First Warm Rain

The first warm rain in early spring can cause great numbers of walleyes to migrate into the headwaters of a river or reservoir system to spawn. This spawning run is most likely to occur at night, and the biggest females are often the first to reach the prime spawning grounds on shallow shoals and riffles. Some of the biggest walleyes ever recorded have been taken this early spring spawning pattern— but it takes a subtle approach. Sneak into casting position with your electric trolling motor and fish a minnow lure slowly through the shallows.

Soft Touch

Most walleye experts prefer rods with a soft tip action. Walleyes often bite tentatively and may quickly reject your lure or bait if they detect rod pressure.

Use Long Rods For Trolling

Walleye specialists user longer rods than most other freshwater anglers—especially for trolling. Many prefer soft- or medium-action sticks spanning 8 to 9 feet in length. Their extra length allows you to cover up to twice as much water with your lures or live baits when trolling.

Target Points First

Main-lake points with a slow taper into deep water are among the most important reservoir walleye structures. These fish will often suspend off the ends of points, where they intercept passing baitfish schools. Points subjected to strong winds can be especially productive.

The Fast Track To Shallow Walleyes

In some lakes and rivers, walleye occur shallow—sometimes under 10 feet. The fastest way to locate these shallow 'eyes is to troll crankbaits. Target the ends of points, submerged humps, sand and gravel bars and weedlines, and, if conditions allow, bang your plugs right off the bottom.

The Question Of Color

The jury is out on which lure colors are best for walleyes. Many anglers point out that creatures that have good night vision (including walleyes) generally have poor color vision. Others argue that walleyes show definite color preferences, and often list perch, fire tiger and blaze orange lures as the hot tickets. You be the judge—experiment with color on your home waters and stick with what works best for you.

To trick a following musky into striking, try figure-eighting your lure at boatside.

NORTHERN PIKE & MUSKY TIPS

Target Shallow Weedbeds

In natural lakes and many rivers, pike and musky show a strong preference for shallow weedbeds. Begin at daybreak casting big, noisy topwater lures over the tops of submerged grassbeds. Large in-line spinners are a good lure choice once the sun gets high; these ride high in the water and are effective around weedy points and isolated grass patches. Large musky jerk baits cast to weedlines will often pull a big fish out of the grass.

Figure-8 'Em

Muskies are notorious for following a lure repeatedly without striking. To turn a follow into a strike, as soon as the lure nears the boat, drop down to your knees and swoosh the rod tip around so the bait runs in a figure-8. This often triggers an instant strike from a following fish.

Dead Bait Savvy

Biologists have proven some of the biggest pike feed on dead bait. Their theory is that these huge fish expend as little energy as possible to feed; rather than chase after live baitfish, they've learned to swim lazily along and pick dead fish off the bottom. A large dead sucker fished on a 3-way rig around a point accessing deep water may tie you into the pike of your dreams.

Flyrod Fun

Fly-fishing for big pike is a fast-growing sport in the northern U. S. Use a stout bass or light saltwater flyrod with a large, brightly-colored streamer fly or chunky bass popping bug and target shallow weed and wood cover. And make sure you're using a wire leader!

The Walleye Connection

When walleyes make their annual spring spawning run into the headwaters of a reservoir or river system, muskies may not be far behind—when the opportunity to do so presents itself, they'll eat small walleyes like candy. Fan-cast a large brown or olive green jerk bait or crankbait around potential walleye spawning areas for a monster musky—and hang on to your rod!

Ice-Out Pike

In the north country, the biggest pike of the season can often be caught just after the ice begins breaking up in early spring.

Shallow flats, ditches and creeks are potential hotspots that can yield a huge pike if you're willing to brave the frigid conditions. Try retrieving a large red-and-white spoon lazily through the icy-cold shallows. Of course, check local fishing regulations for the opening date of pike season.

Troll The Prop Wash

Musky trollers know that a lure such as an in-line spinner or crankbait trolled right in the outboard motor's prop wash will often nail a big fish. Make sure your reel drag is set so it slips a bit when Mr. Musky chomps down on this short-line presentation.

Jerk, Jerk, Jerk

When trolling big diving crankbaits for pike or musky, don't use a rod holder. Instead, keep the rod in your hands and periodically jerk it back sharply. This will cause the lure to suddenly dive or veer off erratically to one side, a good way to trigger a strike from a following fish.

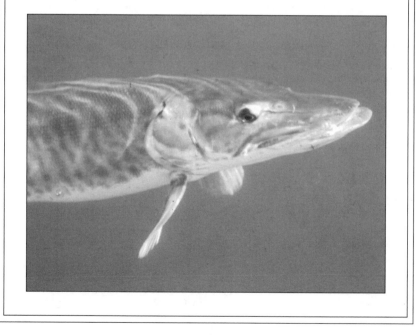

Premium gift books from PREMIUM PRESS AMERICA include:

❖ ❖ ❖

TITANIC TRIVIA

❖

BILL DANCES TREASURY OF
    FISHING TIPS

❖

LEONARDO – TEEN IDOL TRIVIA

❖

GREAT AMERICAN COUNTRY
    MUSIC
GREAT AMERICAN STOCK CAR
    RACING TRIVIA
GREAT AMERICAN WOMEN
GREAT AMERICAN GOLF
GREAT AMERICAN CIVIL WAR

I'LL BE DOGGONE
CATS OUT OF THE BAG

❖

STOCK CAR TRIVIA ENCYCLOPEDIA
STOCK CAR FUN & GAMES
STOCK CAR DRIVERS & TRACKS
STOCK CAR LEGENDS

❖

AMAZING ARKANSAS
ABSOLUTELY ALABAMA
FABULOUS FLORIDA
    (available summer 1998)
GORGEOUS GEORGIA
TERRIFIC TENNESSEE
VINTAGE VIRGINIA

To order or for more information contact:

PREMIUM PRESS AMERICA
P.O. Box 159015
Nashville, TN 37215-9015
(800) 891-7323
(615) 256-8484 office
(615) 256-8624 fax

PREMIUM PRESS AMERICA books are available in bookstores and gift shops everywhere. If, by chance, none are carried in you local area books can be ordered direct from the Publisher. All premium books are $6.95 plus $2.00 for shipping & handling. Quantity discounts are available. Expect delivery in 7-10 days.